Strongman Contest

Strongman Contest

Poems by

Steven M. Smith

© 2021 Steven M. Smith. All rights reserved.
This material may not be reproduced in any form, published,
reprinted, recorded, performed, broadcast,
rewritten or redistributed without
the explicit permission of Steven M. Smith.
All such actions are strictly prohibited by law.

Cover design by Shay Culligan
Cover art by Harris and Ewing

ISBN: 978-1-63980-044-5

Kelsay Books
502 South 1040 East, A-119
American Fork, Utah 84003
Kelsaybooks.com

In memory of my father who told me life is a 7 – 10 split.

Better learn to bowl.

Acknowledgments

Many thanks to the editors of the following publications where some of these poems first appeared, sometimes in slightly different form:

The Akros Review: "Scenes from a Late-Night Movie" (originally titled "Revenge: A Story Poem") and "Dampness"
Chiron Review: "The Visit"
Fox Cry: "Last Supper," "My Stepfather's Eye," and "Clearing the Land"
Kansas Quarterly: "Farewell," "Treasure Hunt," and "Caught"
Lake Effect (Oswego, NY): "The Garage Attic"
Luna Negra: "The Jungle Gym"
misnomer: "Somniphobia"
Mudfish: "Deserter"
New CollAge Magazine: "Polio Pond"
Poem: "A Glimpse" and "Recompense"
Poetry Motel: "Super Bowl Sunday"
RATTLE: "Monopoly"
Reader's Break: "Bill"
Spout Magazine: "Sleeping Over"
Studio One: "Something to Do"
Upstate New Yorker: "Strongman Contest"
West Wind Review: "Bowling Night" and "Second Coming"
Without Halos: "Stealing Cigarettes," "Scrawny Company," and "Hitting the Heavy Bag After Losing My Job to Budget Cuts"

I wish to thank Karen Kelsay and the staff at Kelsay Books for believing in my work. Further thanks to Stellasue Lee, Christopher Citro, and Donna Steiner—writers I greatly admire—for reading my manuscript and providing commentary. And I also want to thank Kenneth Nichols for his generous editorial support.

Contents

I

Rearview Mirror Backhand	15
Scrawny Company	16
Treasure Hunt	18
Caught	20
Escape Reading	21
The Garage Attic	22
Something to Do	23
Thanksgiving	25
Strongman Contest	26
Bowling Night	27
Sleeping Over	28
Polio Pond	30
Stealing Cigarettes	31
Fair Haven Beach	33
Snow Day Lesson	34
Gang Life	36
First Business Kiss	37
Deserter	38
Farewell	39
Last Supper	41

II

Reflections After an Argument with My Pregnant Wife	45
Somniphobia	48
Scenes from a Late-Night Movie	49
First Steps	50
Dampness	51
A Glimpse	52
Clearing the Land	54

October Man	55
Medicine Man	56
Those Winter Mornings	58
My Stepfather's Eye	60
Batting Practice	61
Recompense	63
The Hike	64
The Visit	66
Alcohol	68
Rematch	69
Second Coming	70
Opening Day	71
Visiting My Grandfather	73
Monopoly	75
Coffee, Childbirth, and Aluminum Siding	77
Hitting the Heavy Bag After Losing My Job to Budget Cuts	79
Lesson in Worry	80
Bill	82
Crazy in a July Heat Wave	83
The Jungle Gym	84
Homage to My Workout Room	85
Day One of the Bicycling Exercise Program Sunday 5:00 a.m.	86
Super Bowl Sunday	88

I

Rearview Mirror Backhand

Long before mandatory seatbelts,
I used the back seat of the family Chevrolet
as a wrestling mat to practice Killer Kowalski's dreaded
stomach claw and my own creation—the cauliflower facial.
I still wonder how my sisters' screeches never shattered
the windshield! In the rearview mirror my father's eyes turned
cutting torch blue. In the rearview mirror his brow
and the bridge of his nose crinkled as if he was holding
his bowling ball to his chin—aiming at a 7 – 10 split.
In the rearview mirror the muscles in his cheeks
flexed with the stressful accountability of all the fathers
on the planet. I never saw it coming. He readied
himself, using his version of Killer Kowalski's stomach claw
on the steering wheel. Then the back of his right hand—
a pillow case stuffed with a bowling pin—would blast me out
of the backseat ring into the glass coffin of the rear window deck.
And there I whimpered in embarrassment—not pain—
while my sisters' giggles applauded my temporary defeat.

Scrawny Company

I was a spindle-legged kid
with a xylophone of ribs
that my father tapped
and tickled. My arms
were drumsticks. The hairs
on my head were toothbrush
bristles. I could wedge
a half dollar between
my monstrous front teeth.
I was all elbows and thumbs.
Still my father found pleasure
in my scrawny company. He
twisted me on the bald tire
that hung like a rubber
rocket outside the kitchen
window until my head
bumped the barkless limb;
then he spun me to earth,
while I hung on and screamed
"Mayday!" over the neighborhood
airways. He bounced me
around the house in the wheelbarrow,
while I poked a shovel handle
into the black heart
of a princess-stealing dragon.
He wrestled me long past
my bedtime on the living room
floor until my mother scolded
us on the midnight battlefield
of bleeding popcorn, dead
soft drink bottles,
and crippled furniture.

But a handful of autumns
later, drinking and other
women possessed my father.
So I crawled into the dust
under my bed and curled up
into a bony little ball.

Treasure Hunt

The moon lay flat in the August twilight
like a gold coin surrounded by a googolplex
twinkling dimes, and I jumped from the steps,
but my fingertips kept missing, missing
that immense pirates' chest as well as
the dusky moths that worshipped the yard light.
Mosquitoes shouted in my ears.
The mowed grass tripped up my bare feet.
I caught a toad as it hopped and peed
from the suffocating begonias.
This night while my mother opened
the fitting rooms at Grants department store,
my father sat on the steps
opening beer cans with Mrs. Mooney,
the big lady who lived down the road
next to the old posted landfill.
My father stood and tried to balance
an empty can on the tip of his nose . . .
then two . . . then three, and Mrs. Mooney
giggled and slapped her trembling thighs.
Then my father jumped from the steps
and bellowed, Laaaadies and Geeeentlemen,
and he kneeled, and he pressed
his head to the grass, and he slowly
did a headstand, and as the sparkling
coins fell from his pockets, Mrs. Mooney
giggled and slapped her heavy hips.
And I heard the phone ring and ring and ring.
My father got to his feet, grass
sticking to his reddening face.
His nickels, dimes, and quarters
glistened on the grassy stage.
And the phone was still ringing and ringing.
Then he fired up a cigarette and said,

Tell your mother I'll be there soon,
and he walked hand in hand with
Mrs. Mooney into the backyard's
syrupy darkness, and I ignored
the ringing and the giggling,
and I looted the abandoned lawn
for my father's forgotten treasure.

Caught

One moonless December midnight my father
came home trembling and staggering, holding
a handkerchief over his face.
From the darkness of my doorless
bedroom, I watched my mother
put a hand on my father's shoulder.
He cried at the kitchen table
under the dim stove light,
his shoulders and chest heaving
under his plaid hunting coat.
She combed back his snarly hair
with her fingertips and cradled
his head in the crook of her arm.
She removed the handkerchief from his face,
and I saw blood on his nose and chin.
Oh, Christ, he sobbed. He's here!
And I saw my father's wet and puffy eyes
bulge as a car's lights swung across
the kitchen window, and I heard a wave
of gravel, and then the lights stopped,
and the engine revved to an idle.
A car door cracked open and banged shut.
Oh, God, my father cried. Me and his wife—
And when the kitchen door slammed open,
I buried my senses in my pillow
and tried to imagine just how big
that brook trout was that spit
my hook last spring.

Escape Reading

Brucie stopped spitting.
Richie unclenched his fists.
Eddie put down his kickstand.
Ricky dropped his fishing pole.
Davey tied his sneakers.
Mikey tucked in his shirt.
And I smiled,
there on my front steps
under the shade of the old
glorious sugar maple, opened
my library book to the "Jabberwocky"
and read to my friends.
My root beer Popsicle drooled
like motor oil on the Jabberwock's violent
"whiffing through the tulgey wood,"
intensifying its "eyes of flame."
But "One, two! One, two! And through and
through"—I smothered its burble,
"Callooh! Callay!"
Then I maneuvered my
obedient troops further
and further into the wood,
closer and closer and closer
to Hansel and Gretel,
who were pinned down
by a cannibal lady cackling
in her house made of baked goods.

The Garage Attic

There was only one way up,
up steep stairs that my grandfather
built out of wooden pallets
he found at the town dump.
The entrance was a plywood
trap door guarded by slivers,
cobwebs, and an angry wasp.
When I was up there and safe, I'd slide
my grandmother's crank
phonograph over the trap door.
I'd remove a stolen cigarette
from my hiding spot in the rafters,
and I'd do what a lone boy does best.

Up there I could be a ball turret gunner,
the first boy to kick up dust on the moon,
or a father fishing with his son from a bridge.

Something to Do

I followed my father
around the garage
until he shouted,
"Find something to do!"

So I scuffed the unmowed
grass with the toes
of my bare feet
across the bright back yard
that summer noon,
skipped down the ruts
of the lot car path,
jostled my meandering way
through the pricker patch
into the woods where
the deer flies circled
my head, and then I
waded into the clearing
where the lingering dew
steamed in the shin-deep moss.
There, surrounded by the safety
of sugar maples and Scotch pines,
I stripped in the dusty heat
of the spotlight sun,
while the chickadees
applauded from huckleberry
bush to bush. I got
down and sank into
the damp moss bed.
All around me the breeze
waved ferns big as fans.

I explored the clouds
that floated like
helium-filled mountain
ranges cut off neatly
just above their snowy
timberlines until a
lonely crow called
me back to earth.

Thanksgiving

My stomach remembers over twenty steamy
pounds of bulging turkey, gobbling up
most of the dining room table.
A casserole, big as a washtub,
full of mashed potatoes next
to the bowl of homemade stuffing
with mushrooms. Fresh cranberries,
big as the tip of my father's
thumb, are docked by the gravy
boat. And Grandma's silver
platter is adorned with black
and green olives, celery and
carrot sticks, bread pickles,
and radishes. And over by
the baked acorn squash, there
is a basket of dinner rolls playing
hide-and-seek under a checkered napkin.
I wave my fork like a baton
over the reflection in my plate,
singing "over the river and through
the woods" to my grandmother's
hearing aid, while my mother
leans over the cooling pumpkin
pies, rubs steam from the dining
room window with her apron . . .
and waits for my father
to sober up so she
can help him out of the car.

Strongman Contest

One sleepless summer night
to the coaxing of the crickets'
chant, under the spotlight
of a full moon, my boozy
father sat shirtless on the steps
and flexed for the Big Dipper,
the Dog Star—all the blazing
brawn of the night's center stage.
I waited in an eternal line
just to feel his hairy biceps.
Then I had to arm wrestle
him until my elbow felt
unhinged and my straining
eyes burned to dryness.
He flexed again and the begonias
booed, the moths around
the yard light mimicked, and
the puny bat that swooped
from the garage attic chased
him into the house for the night.

Bowling Night

Now I remember it all—bowling night
with my father: the cheeseburgers
that could fill a catcher's mitt,
the piles of french fries submerged
in ketchup, the salt blinking
under the smoky alley lights, nursing
Coca-Colas in highball glasses,
the bubbles tickling my upper lip,
the bubbles nipping my fingers as I
spear the ice cubes with a straw.
I fly a bomber over the battalions
of pins coming like pawns, as the bowlers
with their beer keg bellies
hurl their cannon balls.
I can see my father biting a cigarette,
juggling a draft, while digging
deeply into a pocket and then pouring
out a handful of linty change for me
to plunk down into the candy machine;
I can hear the *ker-clang* as I yank
the red knob again and again, watching
a galaxy of Milky Way bars fall to earth.

Sleeping Over

That Friday night my mother had to work
a register at Grants department store,
so my father drove me to Richie Mooney's.
When we pulled into the driveway,
the Christmas tree winked in the window.
Mrs. Mooney answered the door.
Her loose bathrobe was wrinkled.
Her freckled cleavage was on display.
Her frizzy red hair was pinned in a bun.
She ignored me and signaled to my father
by holding a beer can up to the yard light. . . .

Richie's snoring woke me at dawn.
The plastic over his bedroom window
suffocated the Saturday sunrise.
I went downstairs to the bathroom.
The kitchen table was scattered beer cans,
glutted ashtrays, crumbled saltines.
Richie's cat was on a chair licking
a plate of hardened Limburger slices.
In the living room, the Christmas tree
had fallen against the wood stove.
Mrs. Mooney's bedroom door was off the hinges.
I looked in and found my father.
He was on his back, hands flopped on his chest.
Mrs. Mooney's head rested on his thigh.
Her drool clung to his leg.
Her freckled cheek was the color of baloney.
I stepped in and held my breath.
My father's mouth was open.
Something made me look into his mouth,
and it was like looking down
into a can of flat black paint.

Then my stomach lurched.
I dressed and ran outside into the woods
and threw up under a clump of sumacs.
The air was warm. But the mid-December sky
was changing like hand-me-down bath water.
The snow in the woods was thick as cold
chicken gravy, but I trudged on toward
home with my queasy secret, with my dry heaves,
with my eyes dripping fear—
my brain already becoming nothing but a whiteout.

Polio Pond

Polio Pond lay like an eyesore
in the abandoned gravel bed on the far
side of the old posted landfill.
There it simmered all summer long
in a horseshoe-shaped depression
surrounded by gravelly cliffs, their tops
littered with sumacs and campfire rocks.
One spring in English class I studied
classical mythology, and that summer
I sat on a marooned bald tire and pondered:
Polio Pond was a mixture of Cyclops'
snot and vomit and a foe's blood.
Maybe I sat in the spot where
Polyphemus clobbered Acis with a rock?
On one side of Polio Pond, the cattails
grew tall as state troopers.
On the far side, where teenage couples
left sticky blankets and slung condoms,
I caught a bullhead with a sharpened stick.
That was the spot where Eddie skipped
a stone thirteen times and broke a beer bottle.
From there Richie once tried to swim
Polio Pond underwater, but he bumped
heads with a snapping turtle big
as a garbage can lid—and nearly drowned.
My father told me not to swim in that pisshole;
he said swimming there caused things:
sinus headaches, nosebleeds, warts, canker sores.
But I only listened to him with earplugs in.
And every summer long that old gravel bed
was my kingdom come.
                                      And every summer long
I would wade into Polio Pond and count
the welts the breeze raised on its surface.

Stealing Cigarettes

When my father got home, he
used a beer bottle to prod
me out of my lower bunk
and into the kitchen light.
I yielded like a condemned
bovine, while I tried
to rub the dirty dream
about Patty Jo Johnson's
sixth-grade breasts out
of my stinging eyes.
My father fired up one
of my stolen cigarettes
and stared out the kitchen
window at the white-cold
moonlight with a combat
soldier's growth on his face.
He removed his thin leather
belt and folded it. Then
he cracked the ripped
back of his kitchen chair
and yellowed stuffing
fell to the linoleum.
When he focused on me,
he had a universe of full
moons in his eyes; he
pointed the beer bottle
to the right, and I
obediently stepped
to the center of the kitchen
and stood, ready.

I held my burning eyes wide
open. And when my father
clamped his heavy hand
on my shoulder, I heard
the midnight freight
train's whistle blow
through the moonlight.

Fair Haven Beach

On the southeastern shore of Lake Ontario,
bathing in a tub of blue sky, I rubbed
noon sun and shards of cooler ice into my skin.
Then I waited for a splash of breeze to take my breath.
Sixth grade was now just a scab.
My towel was a cool sheet tucked
under a mattress of carefully sifted sand.
My half-inflated beach ball was my pillow.
I watched my mother in her aluminum webbed
chaise lounge let the frothy waves
take her work week like driftwood.
She looked up from her paperback
and whispered, "Let this day be
Saturday at noon in August forever."
And the gulls guarded against any trespassing clouds.
And the milkshakes of waves spilled over my feet.
And my mother's whisper lingered
like the fizz from the Shasta colas I sipped
from our bottomless cooler of paradise.

Snow Day Lesson

After our school district shoveled
its way into the list of closings
on the AM radio, I trudged half
a mile through a whiteout in waist-deep
snow to my best friend's house.
Our arithmetic homework was easy:
drifting snow + snow day = dive flips.
His father's aluminum extension ladder
leaned against the back of his house.
It was like trying to shimmy up
a 16-foot icicle. The frozen rungs
tried to yank off our wet mittens
all the way to the top. We clumped
across the roof to the peak in our clumsy
four-buckle boots. I looked over
the edge. At least three toboggan
lengths below was the snowdrift—
a humongous pile of windblown
chalk dust with a hidden agenda.
And for the first time I froze with fright
on the edge of February that school
snow day. My chattering teeth
could've been a maniac pounding
the keys on a manual typewriter.
It was my turn to go first. But I
couldn't go. It was as if each gust of snow
that rocked me—yet grabbed me—
was my father knocking a lunchbox
of stupid out of me. I just couldn't go.
Wuss! Candy-ass! Baldy balls!
My friend nudged me aside, got the toes
of his boots in place on the edge.

Then he dove with snowsuit outstretched
arms and rolled forward in a superb midair
partial somersault, and when he landed
perfectly on his back, I heard the *thud*
of hard-packed snow meeting boy—
not the plush mattress *pooooooofff* of drifted
snow. His breath exploded from him
as if Danny "The Drool" Donovan
whacked him between the shoulder blades
with an unabridged dictionary. And I
still recall only a slight puff of loose snow . . .
like ashes swirling from a doused campfire.

Gang Life

Richie, Eddie, Ricky, Brucie, and I
were there, down in front of the abandoned
gravel bed, revving invisible engines
on our bicycles, passing stolen
cigarettes, blowing smoke rings around
raindrops and flicking the smoldering butts
at the trajectory of Brucie's spit.
The sun was sick that Saturday spring morning.
The sky gurgled and dripped like phlegm.
It was a day destined to stay in the road,
to harass cheapskates who turned off their lights
on Halloween night, to pedal past Mr. Duffy's
bold poodle and coast away on our bicycles
with middle fingers carving the cloud cover.

I was in sixth grade, and I wanted
to make God and all his haloed pals flinch.

But then, Armageddon stomped upon me!

My father skidded up in his pickup
with a cigarette between his teeth,
slid out with his flannel shirt untucked
and the sleeves rolled up beyond the biceps.
He sneered at my gang and belched, trudged up
to me through a mud puddle with his fists on his hips,
and shook his head as he lifted his chin and sighed.

Then he tossed that relentless thumb toward my house.

First Business Kiss

We were both thirteen. When we stepped from the school bus,
she held the three chocolate bars with almonds
like a treble hook inches from my submissive mouth.
She smiled like a vampire before the bitter bite.
She said, You know what you have to do!
I heard her saliva was sump pump water.
I heard her tongue was a hacksaw blade.
Would I slip into the widening crack
of her cold sore, find the center
of the earth, and vaporize?
She could have mowed her eyebrows.
She could have raked the crab grass
out of her frizzy hair—sawed
the poison sumac out of her nostrils.
She could have taken an ice scraper
to her acne—gargled with bleach.
This was the deal: I pasted my mouth
to hers and counted backwards
from ten to one. Then I pushed her
away with a champagne *pop*.
The bus driver ignited the horn.
The school bus exploded—
a big yellow pipe bomb of laughter.
As she ran off giggling, skipping, dancing
to a businessman's bounce,
her flip-flops applauded—
while my first bad transaction
crumbled and melted in my hands.

Deserter

It was beyond my bedtime
when I ambushed my father—
his senses beaten from a binge.
I caught him shaking his hairy
knuckles in my mother's face,
while she whined half-clothed
in her foxhole under the kitchen table.
I was thirteen. And with stolen liquor
on my breath, I bravely entered
the combat zone of that falling house.
I wavered in the kitchen doorway,
grabbed a sponge mop by the handle,
and screamed threats until my
eyes and nose soaked my face.
The sights of his fist now pointed at me.
His beer bottle exploded on the linoleum,
and I caught shrapnel in the shin.
He charged, and I dropped my
weapon, and I ran, jumped
from the steps to the rainy, moonless yard,
and I ran to the road. And as I ran
I heard his steel-toed work boots wallop
the road, and I felt his
silhouette lumbering after me. . . .

Nearly a mile later I climbed
a slippery bank to a vacant lot and got
tangled in a pricker patch of barbed wire,
and there I cowered all night blinded
by the late summer rain until the sky turned
a bluish black. Then I coughed
and whimpered through the soggy prickers on my
hands and knees toward home.

Farewell

The day my mother screamed
my father out of her life,
his single-shot Remington
12-gauge was pulled from
the closet shelf.
The family photo album fell
to the floor, loose pictures
dropped dead like hunted ducks,
and my father grabbed
a box of birdshot and
picked up the family photo album
and went to the back yard
where the last of the October
leaves blew from the maple
my father planted on the
day I was born.
He had me stand next to him
with my lawn rake ready.
He carefully slid a shell
into the barrel, and with one
hand on the stock, he snapped
the barrel into place, cocked
the hammer with his thumb
and yelled, "Pull!"
When he threw the captured years
of family picnics, holidays,
birthdays, reunions into
the autumn air, jammed
the stock into his shoulder,
pointed the bead away from home,

I flinched with my eyes half closed
and waited with my rake
to gather up the leaves,
the dead pictures,
my father's empty shell.

Last Supper

After a late October supper,
my father and I sat alone
at the kitchen table. Lightning
lashed a power pole at the end
of the road, so my father silently
chain-smoked by candlelight
in front of the kitchen window.
I was next to him, scribbling fire
with my little brother's red and yellow
crayons on a paper napkin, all around
the stick figure of a faceless man,
as I watched the lightning rip
through the tarpaper-black clouds
and the flashing reflections
of my father's cigarettes
in the rain-streaked window.
When my father removed the wadded
divorce papers from the napkin holder,
he started to cry; his sprinkling
tears shimmered from the candlelight.
I stopped scribbling and stared
at the side of his wet and weathered
face for a long time before I
took his trembling hand, blew
out the candle, and helped him
to his pickup in the driveway.

II

Reflections After an Argument with
My Pregnant Wife

End of November. Shivering.
Coughing. Pissed off.
I'm plopped on a wooden bench
that's scarred with the names
and dates of long-gone lovers,
watching the Oswego River's
crippling current wallop
a Main Street bridge abutment.
On the other side of the relentless
river—about seven stone throws—
a church tower bell plays
a Sunday morning tune.
But the whacking water
is too loud, and all I hear
is that familiar fire siren
of guilt blaring in my head.
Earlier I gave my wife the finger
and kicked the screen door
and snarled down the sidewalk
into the fog that boiled on my face.
All I wanted was twenty bucks
of the hoarded rent—
a little afternoon billiards,
some beers, some back slapping
with buddies.   Then I think,
this must be how my father
behaved—throw a temper tantrum
over drinking, borrow some
money and vamoose with a carload
of runaway cronies.

So I frown at the spit-like clouds
and cross my arms, thinking
an anvil dropped on my whimpering
head from Heaven's loft
would be best for my wife, for my
unborn son, for everyone
else in my little life. . . .
Now a small fishing vessel
fights upriver, then gives up,
turns, and moves like a paper boat
away with the current. Impatient
gulls are making a racket over
me, making distorted figure eights.
I notice bare, snarly trees
and ragged bushes jutting
from the rock wall along the shore.
The matted, stomped-on grass
under my feet is littered with fallen
leaves. Under the Main Street bridge
plump pigeons in the nooks are telling
me to get my pitiful act together.
Okay . . . watching water swirl
and foam like a rabid mouth
on a day off is stupid.
                              So I stand.

The wind somehow seems comforting.

Those gulls move closer to the lake.

Now I think I hear another
church bell playing.

Now I think I see that
fishing boat coming back.

Now I think I smell the
blue paint in my son's room.

Now I think I feel my
wife's arms trembling at the screen door.

Somniphobia

Snow. Sleet. Freezing rain. Now rain—
striking, randomly tick-tocking the vinyl siding
this entire December morning of insomnia.
I try to thrash away a dehydrated hangover
on the living room couch, still in my
white socks, Wranglers, and flannel shirt,
thinking about the sighing refrigerator:
ice water, leftover chicken wings, white grape juice,
the green beans cemented in margarine,
the uncovered tomato soup that has
a film thick as the morning paper . . .
but I stay shrouded in an afghan
on the couch, adjusting the falling cushions,
groping for the missing remote control.

This must be the anxiety my father felt
and couldn't ignore after binge swilling
with buddies and grabbing the backsides
of foulmouthed women holding pool sticks.
I can see him sprawled on Grandma's
hand-me-down couch with a limp arm
over his forehead, ashtray and cigarettes
and a Tupperware pitcher of water at arm's length.

At 3:45 a.m.—right on schedule—
the stranger who delivers the morning
paper slides by my mailbox in the sanded slush,
while I peek over the back of the couch,
out into the damp, comatose front yard . . .
the heel of my hand heaving on my heart.

Scenes from a Late-Night Movie

"I'll get that bastard. Get that bastard tonight.
Get him right where it hurts," the father says.
He belches, grabs his Chesterfields, his lighter,
Sinks back into the sofa, and plants
His heels with a bang on the coffee table.
"Yup, right where it hurts," he says, lighting up.
He pulls the beer bottle from between his legs and swigs.

It's dusk. The father and his son sit
At the kitchen table.
The father goes over the details again.
There are saltines on the table, a brick
Of Limburger on a paper plate, mustard.
The father cuts an onion into thin slices on a napkin.
The son swallows some beer.
He eats a slice of Limburger with onion.
Outside the kitchen window the full moon lurks
Behind thin moving clouds.
Streetlights in the trailer park are coming on.
It's April. It's still getting dark at supper.
Kitchen lights are on in most of the trailers.
In some kitchens the son can see glimpses of people
And shadows. Faint glimmers of unknown lives.
The father pops a slice of onion in his mouth.
He swallows some beer and sees headlights.
The landlord drives by with the dome light
On in his new Continental.
The father and the son immediately recognize the woman
In the front seat light a cigarette.
"I can't let you do it," the son says.
"Try and stop me."

First Steps

On the blanket my son
picks and pulls
on his pudgy feet—
all googoos and gaagaas.
And my wife and I
are opposing armies
on each side of him—
arguing about the mass
grave of bills buried
alive in the kitchen drawer
near the ancient refrigerator
that groans like a tundra
and needs a pickax
to defrost inside the apartment
that cries for a new roof.
But my son—a cute border
with blonde locks—
cares only about the robins
that are now skimming,
sometimes landing
in the uncut grass
just beyond his
pointing fingers—
not far beyond
his first steps.

Dampness

By the light of an early morning moon
my faint father staggered into my bedroom
in his T-shirt and boxer shorts, kneeled
on the braided throw rug in front of
my lower bunk, and urinated
on the rug and the linoleum.
Another ten-year-old boy's bizarre dream?
But in the morning light I stepped in my father's waste.
Silently, I wiped the floor with the rug and placed
the rug in a grocery bag,
and took it out to the garage,
and buried it at the bottom of a garbage can.

Early this morning I entered my son's room, kneeled
in the darkness on the carpet in front of his bed,
adjusted his stuffed Gumby and Mickey Mouse,
and rubbed his back through the sheet.
I listened for a long time to his tiny breath,
the cleansing drizzle falling from the roof,
and the far away faint thunder.

A Glimpse

It is 9:00 p.m. Late November.
Sleet scratches the vinyl siding
like the stray cat I should not have fed.
The television is watching me.
The stove light is on simmer.
My wife is still serving her life
sentence in a distant banquet room,
anxious to punch out another bout
with hard labor, sighing as she fixes
her reflection in the time clock window.
My son sucks his fingers on my chest,
and I feel his heart the size
of a sport watch race with the wall clock.
The house noises are in concert tonight,
and this couch is front-row-center stage.
The refrigerator and the furnace
are in unison, but my dog curled under
the end table barks in his sleep out of tune.

A quarter mile down the road
the freight train approaches, lumbering
along its steel fault line.
And now a glimpse of my father, returning
from work, clumps across the kitchen
linoleum of my thoughts.
He settles into his kitchen chair,
lights a cigarette, unlaces his oil-stained
work boots with one hand as he
squints to avoid the stinging smoke.
This evening I cannot smell beer
on his breath as he scoops me up
by the elbows and places me
in his kitchen chair by the window.

I watch as he opens the freezer
to dig out a half gallon of ice cream.
I feel the cold burst and watch
the swirling, frosty fog surround him.
He returns to the table with the frozen
treasure and two spoons, smiles,
and ruffles my hair as he winks.

As the freight train rumbles away,
I can still feel my father's sober return.
I can still feel the ice cream melt in my mouth.
I can still feel my body tremble beneath my son.

Clearing the Land

When I stood face to face
with my wooded acre of virgin
land, I proudly revved my used $100
chainsaw—its rattle of herbivorous
teeth forcing the spring leaves
to tremble, trees twice my age
to shudder under a desertion
of cloud cover—I felt it was my
divine right to come and conquer.
I sawed my way through.
When one tree gasped, creaked
and collapsed, I raised a blistered
fist and moved on to another. . . .
Within days I raised my sweaty
T-shirt on a dead limb and looked
down on a continent of stumps,
and I nodded like a cross-armed
dictator from a balcony . . .
and visualized how a full moon
might look kneeling on
the doorstep of my new palace.

October Man

The alarm clock clump-clops
like Boris Karloff's footsteps
on my night stand.
The wind outside my bedroom
window hollers and curses
like a torch-toting mob.
The October leaves bite
the vinyl siding
like vampire bats.
The furnace is a belching zombie.
My son staggers into my bedroom—
a werewolf pup, dragging
his blanket like a tail over
the top of me and then over
the top of my wife,
who is snoring in tongues.
I decide to leave this
classic before the credits.
I scratch my eyes all
the toe-stubbing way
to the kitchen and make
a twelve-cup pot of coffee.
I sit naked in my kitchen chair
biting my fingernails, listening
to the *pa-pooooshhhh*
of the electric percolator.
And I wait for the sun
to smother the twisted
smile of the crescent moon
so I can change back
into a tired taxpayer,
a happy husband,
and fortunate father.

Medicine Man

I escaped from a dream
about a serial killer—
some male nurse who killed
dozens of patients
with lethal injections.
And in the dream the malignant
maniac was after my son
with a needle big
as a shish kebab skewer.
Now I'm awake, dressed
in jeans and socks.
I must've slept on my
shoulder wrong—the one
I dislocated in rugby
years ago. The arthritis
is now gnawing like a trapped
rodent. With the remote,
I turn on the cable station
that has the time; dawn
is three hours away.
It's time for my son's
strep throat medication.
I nudge my wife but she
mumbles, smacks her lips,
and rolls away from me,
knotted in blankets.
I rub my yawning eyes
downstairs, pull open
the front door and squint
at the yard light. Freezing
rain crackles on the crusty
snow. The sky is an ancient
burial vault. I go
to the refrigerator, take

out the bottle of pink
medicine, poke a steak knife
into my hand as I paw
for a teaspoon, scuff up
the stairs in my drooping
socks, cautiously enter my
son's room and step over
landmines of Matchbox cars,
army men, mutant action figures,
assorted building blocks.
I smile when I see my son
wadded up in his plaid
pajamas like fabric
in a remnant bin at Kmart.
His room has that stuffy-sweet
smell of boy. I sit on
the edge of his bed and
whisper his name over
and over and over, until
he opens his filmy eyes,
stretches, and squeaks,
"Hi, Dad."

Those Winter Mornings

This winter morning there's a universe
of black holes in my head.
My wife and I drank too late
with foul company—something we've
been doing too much of lately.
The furnace woke me at five.
My wife's knee in the small
of my back was breakfast.
Later, some coffee in the chipped mug
in my study while I try to rub
the morning paper into my eyes.
That's when my son jumps into my paper to show
me the crumpled dollar
from the Tooth Fairy, but he
can't comprehend why the tooth—
still taped to the back
of the power bill—was left where
it was placed under the pillow.
I think, Too many rum and Cokes will do that.
I look through the mini blinds
and see too much January—
lake effect snow piling up
in the driveway, blowing
across the yard.
I cough into my hand;
I must've smoked a tobacco shed last night.
Now my wife hollers at my son:
he's kicking field goals
in the living room again.
Go watch cartoons! she screams.
Cartoons? I think.

I remember my father's hungover eyes
dripping into my face the Saturday
morning he shook the Sylvester and Tweety
episode out of my head and told
me my grandfather grabbed his chest
and died in his mobile home
in the trailer park
where they allowed kids.
That's when I close the blinds, my eyes,
and wedge a fist into my chest . . .
and try to think about summer.

My Stepfather's Eye

I remember your dead eye.
The eye you said the chicken pox
smothered when you were a kid.
And I remember how I would sneer
at that vacant side of your face,
clench my fists and ease
both middle fingers up
inches from that lifeless—
but sober—socket . . .
because your good eye
had nabbed me during some
delinquent act of teenage disorder.

I now want to apologize
for hating your authoritative guts
and for pouring handfuls of gravel
into the gas tank of your Dodge.
And I now want to say thanks
for your good eye
since my real father's two
runaway, boozy eyes were only
yellow pissholes sizzling
in the snow.

Batting Practice

It's a muddy April.
Out in the back yard
where the leach field's
dark drool smells
like rotten eggs,
I use a paper plate
for home base and a garden
glove for a pitcher's
mound. I know my
son can't swing
straight enough to hit
a slow pitched Volkswagen Bug,
but I patiently
toss the pile of new
baseballs and fight
the forbidden frown
as my son strikes out
six innings in a row.
A quarter-inch sheet
of plywood is the backstop.
It's propped against
the picnic table,
and it's so riddled
from strikes it looks
like a firing squad's wall.
But when I say
I'm tired, my son
steps out of the imaginary
batter's box and spits
like a pro . . .
and when he digs in
at the plate again,

he chokes up a little
more on the bat and hollers,
Just one more, Dad!
One more!

Recompense

One summer my son picked out
a five-dollar rabbit from countless cages
strewn in a crackling barn that leaned
like a kid's forgotten fort.
The farmer placed the black and white,
quivering handful in a disposable
diaper box with some dusty hay, and I
drove home with my son half in the box.
At the lumber store I counted rolled coins,
while a scowling employee cut my sheet
of plywood in two so it would fit in my trunk.
At home I yanked scrap two-by-fours
from the rafters in my garage,
and one dropped and dented my eyebrow.
For two days my claw hammer missed
my thumbnail, but on the third day
to the blare of the rock 'n' roll radio
and after six or seven beers I smashed
the ring finger on my left hand.
A blood blister blew up under my wedding band.
I cursed the inventor of rabbits and kicked
a leg out from under the cage. . . .

But by the end of the fourth day my son's
rabbit had a redwood-stained palace,
and I had my wife's lipstick on my cheeks,
and my son's arms wrapped around my waist.

The Hike

It's the last Sunday morning
of an ark-builder's April:
my sump pump coughed up
too much rain and died;
local flooding has even
brought the governor
nodding and shaking hands.
But this morning the rain
is in remission. This morning
I'm taking my son on a hike.

We walk downhill past
a quarter mile of neighbors
to the railroad tracks, our
walking sticks guiding us
like the wands of wizards:
I can turn that barking
Doberman into a white dove;
my son blows a pink bubble
and says he can change
it into a flying horse
with two saddles.
At the railroad tracks, my son
can't decide which way to go.
So I play the Scarecrow
and lean against the pole
of the crossing lights.
I say, "That way's a very
nice way" and flop
a brainless arm to the right.
For a hundred yards we
tightrope walk the rails,
and it's like walking
the greasy bellies of eels.

Then we poke through the jagged
railroad rocks for treasures:
there's an empty shotgun shell,
a rusty spike, a piece of coal,
a pile of deer droppings,
a blackberry brandy bottle.
Then, a few yards from the tracks,
we find a freight car coupler
in a mossy puddle—its hook
looks like the open mouth
of a huge petrified fish.

Past a barrage of posted signs,
down an embankment of boulders,
across a sandy spot dotted
with deer tracks, a foamy stream
runs through a concrete culvert
into a swampy area of bushes
and tree stumps. And there—
loafing like an old man on his porch—
we see a soaked beaver sprawled
on top of his pile of sticks.
Our eyes ignite, and we
kneel, . . . whisper, . . . and watch—
until we hear our town's
noon whistle blow . . . and our
empty stomachs calling us home.

The Visit

It's nearly midnight
when the doorbell yanks
me out of bed like the SS.
I open the front door
with my son's aluminum
bat on my shoulder.
The yard light
barks in my face.
My wife and son
whisper behind me.
At the bottom of the steps,
my father sways.
He's holding a can
of Pabst to his chest
like a dead man
holds a rosary.
He burps hello and smiles
like a circus geek—
any moment he'll pull
a squeaking rodent
from his plaid hunting
coat and chew its head off.
Should I throw
him silver coins?
His cheeks and eyes
are sunken—a Dachau
prisoner staring
through barbed wire.
There's a cemetery-gray
growth on his face
so thick he'll need
a Weed Eater to shave.

He's still wearing
the Agway feed store
cap he was born in.
Has the booze left him
bald as his retired
bowling ball?
I haven't seen him
in light-years.
The last time he stopped
he was crocked, and I
think he tried to kiss
my wife on the mouth.
Does he know my son
can score touchdowns
on his flag football team
like a union carpenter
can drive straight nails?
Does he know my son
can write words like
"grandfather" in cursive?
Does he know I could
jump on him with this
baseball bat and beat
the meaning of "love"
and "family" into
his sorry soul?

Alcohol

So
I still stand tall
inside my house
with my hands down,
glaring at You through
the screens of open windows.
I see You crouching out
there on a prickly,
weedy pile, licking
Your scythe patiently
as a beast licks a bone,
waiting for me
to come out and
down
to Your kingdom,
done.

Rematch

I'm an adult . . . but for some reason
I'm climbing over the steel fence
that encloses my childhood front yard—
a Tonka bulldozer in one hand,
a G.I. Joe doll in the other.
My father meets me on the roadside
of the fence, belching with mad breath,
searing with asylum eyes—a beer bottle
rests like a baseball bat on his shoulder.
Behind him a slew of neighbors, relatives,
strangers applaud and holler in the bleachers.
This time when my father brings the beer bottle
down on my head, I don't even flinch.
I nail him between the legs with the bulldozer,
poke the head of the G.I. Joe in his eye,
and get him in a headlock: his
Brylcreem and Aqua Velva fuel my rage.
I squeeze and wrench . . . squeeze and yank . . .
while he bawls like a beaten boy. . . .

When I wake, the alarm clock
is shouting at me, and my pillow
is blubbering and gasping and clawing
in the crook of my arm.

Second Coming

My father came this November dawn,
down the neighbor's wheel-rutted path
across the road from my house.
He came slowly floating, the toes
of his new work boots pointing
down, inches above the frost that made
powdered donuts out of the fallen leaves.
He came with his arms wide open,
with his palms outward and washed,
with his plaid hunting coat zipped.
He came sober with his hair cut and combed,
with his face shaved, with his head
to one side, smiling, humming something familiar.
He came through the tunnel of bowing
sugar maples and kneeling weeds—
followed by a congregation of white light.
As he passed the ancient burn barrel
scarred by shotgun blasts and approached
the crisscrossed railroad ties that block
the end and the beginning of that path,
my arms rose to forgive him. But then
I got a whiff of exhaust like I
did the day he drove away,
and his figure dissolved in my hands.

When I woke, my eyes and nose
were running into my hands,
and my son was crying next to my bed,
holding a flashlight in my face.

Opening Day

My wife's snoring
beat the alarm clock.
When I rub my eyes,
I find dried up
night crawlers.
The bedroom is a safe,
and I'm a chained
Houdini, trapped
with no tricks up
my pajama sleeve.
I have to take
my son trout fishing.
At the window I see
the sun hasn't left for home.
Black rain beats
my house like vandals.
In the bathroom,
the night-light
gives me the finger.
The toilet water
wants my soul.
The mirror has the dry heaves.
I begin to grope my way
back to bed, . . .
but then I realize I'm
only heading to the end
of a flat world—
a fathomless sty
where sea serpents
use toothpicks after gnawing
on promise-breaking fathers.

I turn and squeak my son's
bedroom door open and move
to his bed like I'm
fighting an icy current
with waders full of water.
I waver there for a long time.
Then I tell him to get up
before the trout stream
in my conscience
runs out of fish.

Visiting My Grandfather

Easter Sunday morning
in the South Richland Cemetery.
I'm sitting alone in my
station wagon with the engine
off and the window down,
next to the eleven-year-old
grave of my father's father—
my first visit of the year.
No one else is here.
All the snow has melted.
The acres of faded plastic
flowers can breathe again.
But the dead-breath sky
is gargling more rain,
and the wind smells like tossed
handfuls of wet dirt and worms.
I wonder if this morning's sky
looks like the fluid
that drowned my grandfather's
lungs in his hospital bed,
while I was off carousing
with unemployed pals in Florida.
Six shovel lengths from my
grandfather's grave, a fat
robin drops from the ancient
pine tree into a fallen
patch of pine cones, and it
stabs something ripe with its beak.
I think, This place
is an all-you-can-eat
feast for a bird.
I get out of my car
and I hear crows heckle.

I walk to my grandfather's
spongy plot, kneel, and move
a hand across and down
the rocky sides of his
gray monument, as if this act
will make him rise
like a claustrophobic genie.
I let my index finger follow
the indentation of our last
name, and I imagine I'm writing
our name in a new sidewalk. . . .

I stand. Some high
geese get my attention. Then I
hear a choir practice of birds
coming from the dozens
of planet-shaped evergreen
shrubs that orbit the cemetery,
and now rain pats my face
like a used handkerchief.
I pick up a cigar-shaped pine cone,
place it in front of my
grandfather's name, and give
him a twenty-one-gun-salute smile.

Monopoly

My son's the sticky-fingered banker—
a vault of red licorice squeaks
in his mouth. He conducts business
from his wooden chair on his knees,
puffing on a fresh piece of licorice,
clutching his stack of $500 bills
as if the IRS is coming for his
fortune with a giant vacuum cleaner.
I'm responsible for the deeds.
I have the few remaining ones fanned
out like a questionable poker hand
on the dining room table.
I toss a handful of M&M's—
such sweet analgesics—in my mouth
and wash them down with Kool-Aid.
Of course, my son's got the car.
And I got the boot.
He's got hotels like red parasites
from Pacific Avenue to Boardwalk.
And he controls the railroads too.
Landing on Luxury Tax would be
the answer to my prayers.
I just want to go to jail,
not pass Go and stay there;
the jailhouse shower is safer!
Well, I've mortgaged everything,
except my hotels on Cockroach Corner—
Mediterranean and Baltic Avenues.
I'm on Marvin Gardens, and it's my
turn to toss those little evil
squares speckled with black holes.

I land on Chance, and I start to wipe
the sweat of bankruptcy from my face,
but then my son hears me whimper:
"Advance token to Boardwalk."

Coffee, Childbirth, and Aluminum Siding

By 3:00 a.m.—thirteen hours after
the hospital's automatic doors
swallowed my overdue wife and me—
I was in the lounge mumbling
to the coffee machine about my wife's
cesarean section being routine,
while another father-to-be snored
with his head embedded in the wooden
arm of a chair that could tell
maternity ward stories for decades.
My crossing eyes were in labor,
heavy as lodged Siamese twins.
The howling television
in the ceiling corner
was an aborted polar expedition.
The loudspeaker crackled
with Herod's soldiers
rounding up newborns.
The yawning nurses scrambled
in the hall, holding clipboards
with death certificates.
When I tried to swallow
more coffee from the paper cup
with the losing poker hand,
my arm turned into an umbilical
cord, my fingers were quintuplets;
I got a hot flash and jumped,
dumping coffee all over
the crumpled magazines
by the lamp with jaundice. . . .

Now eight years later—I'm strangling
a neck of bills, hollering sideways
with a five-day beard
out the living room window:
my son and a neighbor kid
keep batting foul balls
into my new home's aluminum siding.

Hitting the Heavy Bag After Losing My Job to Budget Cuts

In the mortuary coolness
of my basement where the canvas bag
hangs from the floor joists
like a seventy-pound sleeping bat,
I stand under a dim bulb
that I can't afford to leave on
and patiently mummify my hands
with the Everlast wraps.
My son stays silent
and holds the fourteen-ounce
gloves, while I cram my hands
in—sort of like a mad doctor
plunging into surgical gloves
with the help of a mute
and loyal assistant. Then my
son sits on the basement's
bottom step, holding my cheap
Timex, waiting for the second
hand to strike twelve, . . .
and when he says *ding*
my right cross knocks the first
fat bureaucrat out of the ring
and into a comatose unemployment
line. . . .

Lesson in Worry

I'm sick. It's 5:00 a.m.
First Saturday in June.
Damn, I couldn't sleep:
sinus medicine kept me
thrashing in my straitjacket
of wet sheets, while my
mind was a buzzing blender
of mortgage payments,
utility bills, auto loans;
strangers in three-piece suits
and black hoods were taking
axes to my credit cards;
budget cuts were tearing at my
career's carcass like buzzards.
I'm sitting on a Coleman
cooler in my garage
with the overhead door
wide open, looking out
at my unmowed front yard
with its shaving cream of dew,
with its skitter of robins.
There's calm sunlight arousing
the yawn of maple tree shadows.
I'm listening to the early birds—
a private concert in my
one-acre kingdom, and I
show my thanks by slouching
and moping on my cooler throne.

As a kid I recall my father's
face wrinkled with worry.
The garage was his hermitage.
He would lean against his
workbench for hours drinking,
smoking, grumbling, and whining.
He held a fist more than a hammer. . . .

Ahhh, to hell with sinus
infections, bellyaching over
spilled bills, and dwelling
on winding unemployment lines.
I'm going to wake the house:
the diner at the end of my
road still has an all-you-can-eat
breakfast special.

Bill

Some say he has loose
shingles on his head.
Others say his brain
only got half baked.
Maybe too much moisture
in his crawl space.
Or a monkey wrench got
wedged between his ears.
And once an old drunk
on the stool next to you
said Bill was a P.O.W.
See, the Nazis broke
his yolk—left him
a scrambled egg. . . .
But Bill seems uniquely
human to you— like God's
kiss smolders between
his eyes. You think
about this when you
see him around town,
babbling on his bicycle,
his wobbly smile
so genuine it gleams;
or when you see him just
standing on the corner
by the only traffic light,
blurting hello and waving
to the tunnel vision
of rush-hour traffic . . .
like your town's guardian
angel in disguise.

Crazy in a July Heat Wave

At noon the riding
lawn mower throws
a rod—a dead elephant
with a spear through its heart.
I'm barefoot
in the middle
of the front yard,
ankle deep in uncut grass,
dizzy from swatting
deer flies.
I tear off
my sweat-drenched T-shirt
and pound
the hairy jungle drums
on my chest
with tight fists
and let out
a Tarzan holler
that would even send
the Tasmanian Devil
squealing into a hole,
while Jane and Boy
peek out the window
of our aluminum-sided hut,
hoping the neighboring
tribes don't call
the medicine men.

The Jungle Gym

I built it in the back yard
out of pressure-treated
lumber, sweat and swear words,
six gallons of black coffee,
five tubes of pain
relieving rub,
four bottles of aspirin,
and a box of bandages.
With the table manners
of piranha, the jungle gym
devoured three paychecks
and fed a hundred thousand
sizzling mosquitoes.
And now—the work complete—
I stand with my arms
crossed and frown
in the shade and watch
the different birds
that stop and sing
on my masterpiece,
while my son imitates
a chimpanzee in the maple tree
over my head.

Homage to My Workout Room

Down here in my basement
there's a flex of fluorescent
lights and the psyched grunt
of FM rock 'n' roll. Down here,
where my Olympic weight lifting
bench serves as a shrink's couch,
I come—especially after life's punks
corner me in an alley of debts,
chase me into an abandoned
warehouse of career worries,
drive at me in a street van
of parental paranoia.
When I pick up my curling bar,
I can curl the weight of every
negative thought that ever
existed out of gravity's grasp.
When I jump on the seat of my
lat machine, I can pull pissed off
black holes out of the universe
and rep them ten times—
for an eternity of sets.
Down here I can lift Atlas
with one hand, while the sky
is still on his shoulders.
Down here Hercules hollers
"Sir, yes, sir," salutes,
and fetches my water.

Day One of the Bicycling Exercise Program Sunday 5:00 a.m.

My ten-year-old son detonates
a coach's whistle in my snoozing ear—
right as my picture is snapped
holding a ten-million-dollar lottery check.

Fully dressed in sweats
and Little League cap, my son
greets me at the kitchen table—
a bowl of yawning Wheaties
mumbles good morning.
The bruises on the sliced bananas
float in the skim milk
like the black bags under my eyes.
My head—that boulder with a brain—
begins to topple into my
canyon of cereal, but my son's
whistle in my ear keeps me
on the cliff edge of my chair.

In the bathroom I rub
an abandoned attic
of crusty critters from my eyes;
I choke myself in a noose
of waxed dental floss;
my toothbrush scrapes across
my puffy gums like a rusty file;
I slap my face with handfuls
of cold water and something
in my bad shoulder cracks
like an old tree laden with ice.

I adjust my damp underwear
all the way to the living room
window and find my son already
in the driveway, honking
the horn on his bicycle,
straddling a fresh mud puddle
that's still crowing the reflection
of the sinking full moon.

Super Bowl Sunday

Down! . . . Set! . . . My son spits out
a wad of bubble gum big as a linebacker's
fist. . . . Hike! He goes deep:
ten . . . twenty . . . thirty yards,
while I scamper to avoid our black Lab's
barking blitz, and then I fire the football
through the Sunday autumn breeze, and it
rises into a defense of falling leaves, rises
toward hundreds of cheering black birds
that suddenly explode from the mountainous
bleachers of maple trees that surround
our yard, and it rises into the cold,
sunless sky, . . . but when it drops
back toward earth, it loses its spiral,
wobbles, turns a few lopsided degrees
to the right and begins to tumble
toward my son's relentless stride,
toward his chapped, outstretched hands,
toward his gun smoke breath,
toward his wide-open, runny eyes,
and when the football topples into his arms,
it bounces up into his chin, as he trips
over a cheating tree root and skids headfirst
across the artificial turf of wet leaves;
so I call pass interference as the football
rolls out of bounds into a snarling
patch of prickers and booing weeds.
That's when all those black birds return
to our stadium of maple trees, screaming
and applauding, while my son smiles,
limping back to our next huddle.

About the Author

Steven M. Smith was born in Syracuse, New York. He was raised in a rural area a few miles north of the Village of Central Square, New York. He earned an MA from Binghamton University and a BA from the State University of New York at Oswego. He taught first-year writing as well as reading and study skills for many years at the State University of New York at Oswego, where he is presently the director of the Writing Center. His poetry has appeared in publications such as *RATTLE*, *The Worcester Review*, *Ibbetson Street Press*, *Better Than Starbucks, The American Journal of Poetry,* and *Mudfish*. *Strongman Contest* is Smith's debut collection. He lives with his wife in North Syracuse, New York.

www.ingramcontent.com/pod-product-compliance
Lightning Source LLC
Chambersburg PA
CBHW032010080426
42735CB00007B/554